'HAWKSHEAD R   ˍˍˍ ᴅ'

A WALK IN TIME THROUGH HAWKSHEAD

BY JOHN DIXON

Cover: Flag Street, Hawkshead 1890
Back Cover: Church Stile 1880s
(Mr D Thompson) Mr M Davies Shiel and Dr J D Marshall

Dedicated to the people of Hawkshead
so that our social history may not be forgotten

Published by Helm Press
10 Abbey Gardens, Natland, Kendal, Cumbria LA9 7SP
Tel 015395 61321

Copyright John Dixon and Helm Press 2000

First Published 2000
Reprinted 2004

ISBN 0 9531836 5 3

Typeset in
Baskerville 9pt & 11pt

Typeset and printed by Miller Turners Ltd
The Sidings, Beezon Fields, Kendal, Cumbria, LA9 6BL Tel: 01539 740937

CONTENTS

INTRODUCTION

Welcome to Hawkshead and in particular to this book entitled 'Hawkshead Revisited'. I am a local historian born and bred in Hawkshead. My family has lived here for many generations, either in Hawkshead or within the Parish.

A few years ago when I ran a small Heritage Centre and was conducting guided tours of the town, I realised that there was a definite requirement for a guide book. People were arriving who were frequent visitors to Hawkshead but had never wandered through its many nooks, alleyways, hidden squares and streets, assuming that they would be trespassing on people's private property. This book has been compiled and based on those guided tours to open up Hawkshead to the general visitor and those with an interest in our ancient market town.

> People come, people go
> They take a look
> But still don't know
> What makes us tick
> What makes us smile
> Enjoy yourself
> And stay awhile!

Besides many previously unpublished photographs, there is a lot of information included here that until now has not been common knowledge. I have found that being a local has its advantages, much of my information has come from private local sources, wills, deeds, indentures and photographic collections. The information contained is as accurate as my sources so please excuse any slight error I may have made along the way.

My book is designed either to be read and kept as a history to Hawkshead or as a guide whilst walking round. It only remains for me to thank all those who have so far contributed to my archive collection, thus enabling the publication of this book. In particular I would like to thank, Mrs E Ingham, Mrs E Jay, Mr J West, Mr R Shuttleworth, Mr & Mrs M Wildau, Mr R Fowkes and Dr J D Marshall. Whilst every effort has been made to trace all copyright holders, I apologise to any holders not acknowledged and would be grateful to be be notified of any correction to be incorporated in future editions. Please now take a walk with me and sample the delights of Hawkshead!

John Dixon
Spring 2000

HAWKSHEAD
(1996)

N

KEY

1. Old School House
2. Grammar School
3. Sun Inn
4. Barn Studios
5. Brown Cow Cottages
6. Queens Head Hotel
7. Beatrix Potter Gallery
8. Red Lion Hotel
9. Doctor's Surgery
10. Black Beck Lodge
11. Green Bank
12. Garage
13. Ivy House Hotel
14. Ann Tyson's Cottage
15. Wee Cottage
16. Flag Cottage
17. Minstrels' Gallery
18. Market House
19. Bookshop
20. Kings Arms
21. Spout House
22. Pillar House
23. Wordsworth House
24. Church of St Michael and All Angels

A. Church Hill
B. Slater's Yard
C. Berkley Square
D. Flag Street
E. Vicarage Lane
F. Leather, Rag and Putty Street
G. Main Street
H. Red Lion Yard
I. Market Square
J. Victoria Street
K. Red Lion Square

HAWKSHEAD - HICKEY TURNINGS TO QUEENS HEAD HOTEL

We start our stroll through old Hawkshead at Hickey Turnings, a local name for the road junction on the Hawkshead to Newby Bridge road, to the south of the town. Standing with your back to the town, facing Hannikin and Esthwaite Lake, on the right-hand side of the road we have today's primary school, Esthwaite County Primary, built in 1971, which provides education for the younger children of Hawkshead and surrounding villages. Before the school was built this land was a garden allotment area for the local towns people and in part was a small rural Council Depot. Further along on the right, we can see Spring Wood, a modern housing development built for local people and completed in 1995. On the left-hand side of the road are Hawkshead playing fields and public play area, formerly two fenced off fields but converted in the 1920s to the present recreation ground.

Looking east, we have the main road to Sawrey and the Windermere Ferry. Near Sawrey was the one-time home of Beatrix Potter. This is also the road to Colthouse which was once a thriving Quaker community. The woodland directly behind Colthouse is called Spring Wood from where the nearby housing estate gets its name.

Church Stile in 1880s - note both schools - earlier building on left built 1860 and the school on the right in 1870   *(Mr D Thompson) Mr M Davies-Shiel and Dr J D Marshall*

Old School House

Turn north and face the town. On the left you will notice a barn and farmyard area. This was originally part of the Grammar School, as was most of the land on the southern side of Hawkshead. Next to the barn, moving north, we find the Old School House, this building is still owned by the Grammar School Trust and is used as a small, family run Bed and Breakfast establishment. Originally this was a masters' lodgings for the Grammar School and was also used in part as a lodging house for some of the school boarders. Many's the tale this building could tell!

Main Street (Church Stile)

The main road from Hickey Turnings, towards the centre of Hawkshead, is today known as the Main Street but was originally called Church Stile. As we progress forwards some two hundred yards and look left, we come to the Grammar School itself.

Grammar School

The Grammar School of Hawkshead was built in 1585 by Archbishop Edwin Sandys but because of his death in 1588, it was completed by his son, Samuel Sandys. The letter of patent under Queen Elizabeth I is still to be found at the Grammar School. Today the Grammar School is better known as the house of learning for the young William Wordsworth. In its heyday it was the equivalent of Eton or Rugby. It must be said that this was not the case all of the time, as in the 18th and early part of the 19th centuries, it had declined into a terrible state of affairs from which it never fully recovered.

When originally built the Grammar School was extremely prosperous, owning land not just here but all over the country, though mainly in Yorkshire. It owned property in Trumflett, Bramwythe, Mosely and Sandal, with houses in Kirkgate and Northgate, Wakefield. There were also properties closer to hand, at least five tenements in Finkle Street, Kendal, which were known to bring in each, an annual rent of 53s 4d (approx £2.67).

Along with all the land and buildings on Church Stile in Hawkshead town, there were one or two other cottages in Hawkshead which appear to have belonged to the Grammar School (according to documents in the Lancashire Records Office) but these

Hawkshead Grammar School (Wordsworth's school) about 1910, with the church in the background

have long since disappeared. All we have to go on are house names, so it would be impossible to pinpoint their exact position in the town.

It is worth noting here that rent collection was to be carried out by the school governors and it meant travelling on horseback to each of these individual properties, in midwinter not such a pleasant task. Later on, it would seem that some of the aforementioned properties were sold and the monies received used to purchase more land nearer to Hawkshead, such as Charity High (the large fellside to the west of the town), part of Gallowbarrow to the north of the town, where they built a poorhouse and land near to the Old School House, known as Sark Slieve.

At one stage in 1789, a tutor at the Grammar School, Mr Mingay, tried to open up a Military Academy here. He is mentioned in the Parish Registers and is described as a 'Dancing Master'. The subjects he intended to teach covered the following: English, Latin, French and Greek, writing in all hands, arithmetic, merchants accounts, geography and the use of globes, dancing, fencing and music. Some of these subjects were to be covered by the Grammar School itself but the remainder taught by Mr Mingay. All at the cost of £25 per year, with three guineas entrance fee on top. It is not definite whether this idea of Mr Mingay's actually got off the ground.

The above points must be taken as only a brief description of the Grammar School and for those of you who have an interest in the workings of the school and the involvement of William Wordsworth, a visit is strongly recommended.

Towards the top of the hill, past the Grammar School is the old main entrance to the churchyard and Hawkshead Parish Church. The Church shall be covered later on.

Hawkshead's Main Car Parking Area

Retrace your steps back to the Main Street and facing you is Hawkshead's main car park and tourist trap area. Up until around the 1950-60s all this area was green fields, although the very first shop on this site appeared much earlier. It stood where the landscaped area is today.

It was built and paid for by the Hawkshead branch of the Royal British Legion to provide an income for one of our disabled veterans from the First World War, James Murphy who had been severely wounded in the back by machine gun fire. Much later on Hawkshead's first car park appeared and after being enlarged it was joined by a large café and restaurant called the 'Norseman', this stood on the site of today's large shop, 'Hawkshead Sportswear'. About the same time came the public toilets, bus shelter and an art gallery, known as the 'Barn Studios'. Today on this site is one of the shops owned by Stewardsons of Hawkshead with an adjoining café. Originally the building was a stable area for the Grammar School.

Shortly after the First World War, the roadside opposite the shop was the site of a captured German artillery piece. Although a photograph is in the possession of the author, the original gun has long since disappeared and its whereabouts unknown.

Hawkshead's First School

Just across the road on the left is Hawkshead Tourist Information Centre. This has been built into what was the old school playground gifted by Colonel Sandys in 1885. The playground itself has been made into a small residents' car park. Opposite this car park was Hawkshead's first purpose-built school in 1863 and today is the

Main Street, Hawkshead - 1920s. Old school on left again and on the right James Murphy's shop

Mike and Gill Wildau

Wednesday Club where old-age pensioners meet. The second school was built ten years later, in 1873, opposite the old schoolhouse and is now a pre-school playgroup.

The old school/Wednesday Club was not the first building on this site, prior to 1863 a blacksmith's shop stood there. It was about the same length as the school but it extended into the middle of the road. The blacksmith's smithy actually belonged to the building next door, the Sun Inn. The local guides and brownies group now meet in the old school.

Sun Inn

The exact date that the Sun Inn was built is hard to define but mid to late 16th century could be about right. The original property looked a lot different then to what it does now. Back then, the main building was oblong in shape and set back from the road about twenty feet, with a rising slope leading up to the front doorsteps. The Sun Inn had been built on land belonging to the Grammar School and as such a ground rent and tenancy had to be paid to the Grammar School Governors.

Prior to 1720 little is known of the deeds of occupancy but around this date it was known to have been tenanted by a Mr George Walker, who had successfully applied to the Grammar School Board of Governors to extend the original building at his own cost. Mr Walker besides being the tenant landlord also owned a smallholding and had applied to build a barn and the smithy on the left of the main building and to the right a separate dwelling house for himself and his family - today the Sun Inn café.

On 6th January, 1720 George Walker left the Sun Inn and between then and 1801, the Sun Inn had six different tenant landlords. The 6th January, 1720 was a bad day for the owners of the property - the Grammar School and its governors. The governorship of the Grammar School at that date was not exactly doing its job. The rent for the property at that time was twelve shillings (60p) per year and after George Walker left, someone or some persons failed to collect any rent not just for a short period but right up until 1826.

Evidently one of the innkeepers following George Walker had realised that if and when the rent money owing was collected they would end up in dire straits. To prevent this they had some deeds drawn up (illegally) and sold the property on.

In 1801 the Sun Inn was bought by Mr Thomas Ladyman, who in 1818 willed the property on to his son, George and his wife, Sarah Ladyman. Sarah seemed to be more literate than George as she was the one who signed the deeds. They lived there quite happily and the business must have prospered very well.

But by 1826 the Grammar School accounts were in a terrible shape and the Church Commissioners were called in to revise the situation. On realising that no rent had been received for the Sun Inn property for quite some considerable years, they decided to approach the then supposed tenant, Mrs Ladyman for the back rent owing.

Naturally Mrs Ladyman was not amused and produced her 'deeds of ownership' to prove the property was rightfully hers. To cut a long story short the whole issue was resolved in the High Courts, in London and the case was proved in the favour of the Grammar School but because of extenuating circumstances, Mrs Ladyman had nothing to pay as long as she vacated the premises immediately.

By all accounts the Sun Inn at that time must have been quite a profitable business, for the Ladymans had secured enough money to buy the Queens Head Hotel further along the road. The new tenant at the Sun Inn was Mr Richard Jackson, who was also a farmer and the rent charged was £35 per year.

As a point of interest before we leave the Sun Inn, the author's great-grandfather, Mr James Airey was the landlord just after the turn of the century. A great friend of his, who used to frequent the Sun Inn, was Beatrix Potter and in one of her books, 'The Tale of Mr Todd', is a sketch of the original kitchen. Today it is the lady's toilet in the public bar.

Hawkshead Art Gallery (Barn Studios)

Just up the road on the left-hand side we pass Hawkshead Art Gallery, the new 'Barn Studios'. (Barn Studios as previously mentioned was located near to the main car park and was owned by the art gallery before they moved into their present building). This building was built sometime in the early 18th century but was doubled in size some hundred years later, with a large extension added to the rear, nearer the Sun Inn. Originally known as Church House, this building was also the property of the Grammar School. During the late 1890s it was renamed Esthwaite House and at the turn of the century it was owned by a Mr George Parsons, one of our three town doctors. By all accounts he was a man of considerable wealth, he also owned the pink building on the opposite side of the road and he used this as his surgery. A large, walled kitchen garden lies behind the surgery. Where the shops are today and directly across from the Gallery, was a barn and stable area where he kept his horses. Today this is a woollen shop. In 1903 when the Brown Cow Inn came up for sale, he also bought this and turned it into two dwelling houses. As a point of interest for Beatrix Potter fans, one of her animal characters, 'Johnny Town Mouse' was based on Dr Parsons.

'Old Brown Cow Inn' and Brown Cow Cottages

Carrying on along Main Street we find on the right the 'Brown Cow Cottages'. The first cottage has always been a dwelling house but the two further along were converted from the Old Brown Cow Inn. Tucked in behind the cottages is a small private yard with another two houses hidden from view. These were converted from barns, stables and outhouses belonging to the Brown Cow. Again the age of the Brown Cow is uncertain but a pillar in the sitting room, formerly the bar, bears carved dates from the 17th century. Presumably carved there by past patrons of the inn. There is also a small opening light in the sitting room window from which many flagons of ale would have been passed out to thirsty customers outside. The interior of the building has changed little over many years and has hardly been altered at all. The inside walls are made of oak panels and for the main seem original, with the possible exception of the stud walls, added when the building was altered in 1903. Nearly all the timber work has been fixed with wooden pegs and hardly a metal nail can be seen.

In 1792 the Amicable Society of Hawkshead was formed and continued right up until 1890. At first, the meetings were held in the main Assembly Rooms of the new Market House but by 1819 they were held in the Brown Cow Inn. The landlord at that time was Mr Giles Boulton. The Boulton family had owned the inn for many years from the 1760s to at least 1819, the property having been passed from father to son. Although owners of the inn, the family trade was that of a tailor, so it could be assumed that the family business was also carried on from there. (The Bolton family also mentioned in this book are related to the Boultons).

Points of interest - 'Hawkshead Main'

Now the Brown Cow has two curiosities concerned with it and the first is cockfighting. In 1849 cockfighting was made illegal in England but in this area as well as all over the country it had been classed as a sport and had a great following in and around Hawkshead. A cockfighting match was called, 'a main' and in 1849, 'Hawkshead Main' was done away with, so the so-called 'sport' had to go underground. But in Hawkshead this was not strictly true, a new illegal 'main' was established in the Brown Cow Inn, not actually downstairs, it was carved or scratched out on an upstairs floor within the pub. But how long it was allowed to continue is not known.

'Haaksids Girt Clog'

The second curiosity concerning the Brown Cow is 'Haaksids Girt Clog'. It is in fact a shoe made for a local gentleman of Hawkshead. It measures 20 inches (51 cms) in length, 8 inches (20 cms) in width across the bottom, 16 inches (40 cms) across the front from welt to welt and a heel measuring 7 inches (18 cms). This was made in 1820 for a man called John Waterson, a farmer and tanner by trade, he was also the town mole catcher and as he was one of our church sidesmen, quite a respected man in the area. Unfortunately, he contracted a form of 'elephantiasis' and his left foot was greatly disfigured. In those days if you could not work, you had little or no money, you could quite easily find yourself in the poorhouse but being well known and well-liked and a church sidesman, a local cobbler called Mr John Rigge from Outgate, took pity on him and made him this unusual piece of footwear.

Haaksid's Girt Clog at the Brown Cow Inn 1880s (now in Queens Head Hotel)

Thanks to this piece of generosity Mr Waterson was able to carry out his duties, public or otherwise and indeed he lived to quite a good age. On his death, his wife approached the then landlord of the Brown Cow, Mr Benjamin Usher and said, "Although hę wer' wed t' me he spent ow' his married life t' thee, tha cen hev't clog as a keepsake." So the clog was put in a glass case and left on display. Today alas the Brown Cow has long since gone but the clog can still be seen in the Queens Head Hotel next door.

Victoria Street (Pluck Alley)

The road that runs down to the right next to the Brown Cow Cottages, is called Victoria Street and also has the nickname of 'Pluck Alley'. It is one of Hawkshead's three private roads and the ownership belongs to the main cottage of the old Brown Cow Inn. Today the road leads down to a new housing estate built in the 1980s, known as Kings Yard. It was always presumed that other buildings had previously existed on that site and when the ground was cleared foundations to at least five buildings were found. It is generally thought that these were demolished sometime in the 17th century. Here Victoria Street ends as there is no access into Kings Yard at this point.

The Croft

At the bottom of the street on the right is a property called the 'Croft', built as a farmstead in the mid 18th century, it has now been converted into holiday flats.

Opposite the Croft there is a row of small cottages built around the same date. Just behind these cottages lies the old farmyard complete with all its original buildings but like the town slaughterhouse, which was also situated here, most have been converted into dwelling houses.

Queens Head Hotel

Turning around and heading back to the Main Street, on the right we have the Queens Head Hotel. This is a 16th century property with the exception of most of the bar area, this building has also been altered greatly. Today most of the buildings directly to the rear form part of the hotel but used to be barns and stable area. Most of these were altered in the early 1900s. On Victoria Street, set back into what is now the kitchen area of the hotel was a public weighbridge, which was just big enough to take a small horse drawn-cart and was available for anyone to use.

Besides being the present holder of 'Haaksids Girt Clog' the Queens Head has a few other tales to tell. One is of the death of a small local child, young Alexander Hewitson. The following is from an original notebook belonging to the late Mr Thomas Bradley and written in 1850:-

"An acrostic to little Alexander Hewitson, love of Myles Hewitson of Hawkhead; who was killed March 21st 1850 by a cartwheel falling on him."

The inquest into Alexander's death was held in the Queens Head, the landlord and landlady were Mr and Mrs Ladyman, formerly of the Sun Inn. The cartwheel had belonged to a Mr William Satterthwaite, whose grandson of the same name became the innkeeper of the Queens Head in 1912.

LABURNHAM STREET TO THE RED LION INN

Laburnham Street

Directly opposite the Queens Head, between it and the Market Square is Laburnham Street, which got its name from the large building on the left, which is today a bookshop but was formerly known as Laburnham House. Originally this street was completely residential but it started to be converted into business premises after the 'great fire' of 1846 (I shall mention this in more detail later).

Market Square walking back to the Queens Head Hotel

At this point we shall deal with the right-hand side of the street only, starting at the Market Square and working back to the Queens Head Hotel on Main Street. Originally there were three houses here, the one at the top was the first to be altered, it was owned by the Bolton family who moved in shortly after the fire and they converted part of the house into a grocer's shop. Although they later sold the building to Hawkshead Co-Operative Society, the family remained sitting tenants right up until the 1960s, the tenancy being passed on from father to son.

Bank House (Whigs Café)

Little is known about the earlier occupancy of the central house except that at the beginning of this century it was owned by the Wright family who sold it on to a banking company. They had bought it with the intention of turning it into a small rural bank but one week later better premises became available and the idea fell through. The author's grandparents then purchased the property and changed its name to Bank House, this was in fact the author's birthplace, on 17th March 1957. During the 1970s-80s both properties were knocked into one and used as a bakery but today it is another of our seven cafés and is known as 'Whigs Café.

The name Whigs comes from an old Lancashire form of bread. There are many versions of the recipe for 'Seed Whigs' which is made with caraway seeds but the original recipe for Hawkshead Seed Whigs disappeared with the last local lady to make them, Mrs Mary Noble at the turn of the century. The recipe was classed as a trade secret and died with her but in saying that, the Seed Whigs of today are probably just as good as Mrs Noble's originals. The name whigs has several different variations in its spelling but Wiggs, is used by Samuel Pepys and quoted by H S Cowper in his book, 'Hawkshead (The Northernmost Parish of Lancashire): Its History, Archaeology, Industries, Folklore, Dialect, written in 1887.

The present owners of the third building, nearest to the Queens Head Hotel are the National Trust. Again formerly a dwelling house but has been partly used as a shop since before the turn of the century. In the main this building is stone built but a red brick extension has been added to the right-hand end at some point.

Chemist/Post Office (Noble's Cottages)

Moving on through the town, past the Queens Head Hotel we arrive at Hawkshead's chemist, Post Office and paper shop. This building was built in 1887 by a man called Nathan Garnett. To enable Mr Garnett to build the property, two of Hawkshead's oldest cottages had to be pulled down. They were generally known as Noble's

Nathan Garnett standing at the front door, next to Post Office and Grocers in early 1900s

Cottages and were owned by that local family. The furthest cottage came out at an angle into the Main Street. The second one was built in line with the Queens Head Hotel, directly facing what is known as Thimble Hall. The foundations of this second cottage form the foundations of today's Post Office and chemist's shop. So far as is known only one picture exists of the building and nothing of the second, except a clue to its original lie on the ground using chimney stacks and shadows to plot its position and from photographs of that time.

In other old photographs, two gateposts can be clearly seen which formed an entrance into a throughway which led into the slaughterhouse yard behind the main building. Only one of these gateposts still remain and it stands against the northern wall of the Queens Head Hotel. The paper shop section of today's building is a later addition. It is known that in Mr Garnett's day, this was basically an open ended extension where he kept horse-drawn carts, gigs and carriages. The only other entrance to the slaughterhouse could have been Victoria Street and as that had always been private, this other route would seem the most logical. When the property was first built in 1887, it was split into two separate parts - where the Post Office is today was Mr Garnett's living accommodation and what is now the chemist's was used as his shop.

Thimble Hall

Directly opposite the Post Office we find Thimble Hall, like so many buildings in Hawkshead, it has been knocked about and altered over many years but since the National Trust acquired the property from Beatrix Potter in 1943, it has been kept relatively the same without too much alteration work having been carried out on it Because of the various alterations it is difficult to date the property but it could well date back to the late 16th, early 17th centuries, going by the jetted frontage but even this has been slightly altered. The upstairs windows are typical of late 17th century windows but these could have replaced older ones.

Thimble Hall is not its original name but came into use in the 19th century. Prior to the 1850s the building was an Alms House but after 1850, it was owned by the Hewitson family (relatives to the author). Myles Hewitson was a master shoemaker whilst his wife was a seamstress, as both trades employed the use of a thimble, it was given the nickname 'Thimble Hall'. It is just as well that this trade name stuck, as the next occupant was a Mr Joseph Barker, a local coal merchant - better Thimble Hall than 'Nuttyslack Hall'!

Hawkshead Co-Operative

The building adjoining Thimble Hall to the right is today Hawkshead's Co Operative shop but this was not always so. It was built in 1732 as a large private house and during the latter part of the 19th century it was owned by a Mr Joseph Campbell who allowed the newly formed, Hawkshead Co-Operative Society to use part of the building in 1880 as their shop and then selling the complete building to them around 1915. Looking through the sale documents gives a good insight into what the building either had been used for or what had originally been on the site previously. There i a list noting all the uses that 'must not' be carried out on the premises, including that of a tannery or a tallow chandler - as both these trades needed quite a bit of workspace It might be presumed they were trades carried out prior to the building being erected

Thimble Hall on the left, and building facing on right is Mary Hawkriggs baker/confectioner's shop with 'Bend or Bump' on immediate right in late 1890s

The private house had two entrance doors, one at the front and one at the side of the building facing the present Post Office. Upstairs at the back was a workshop area used by three local cobblers, with a loft door complete with pulley attachment for hauling up the rolls of leather. This also faced the present Post Office. It is known that Mr Garnett who built the Post Office complained bitterly that the shoemakers could look directly into his upstairs rooms but it was pointed out to him that the cobblers had been in operation long before his property had been built, so he lost his argument!

Around the corner of the Co-Operative building nearer the Kings Arms Hotel, there is a small jetted roof which hangs out over the road. This was the site of the very first Co-Operative shop which had three windows and a door facing the Kings Arms. At night, if you stand underneath the archway with the light from the Kings Arms kitchen shining on the wall, you can still see the outlines of these openings, long ago blocked up, but visible underneath the pebble-dash wall. Just to the right of this jetted roof is a flight of stone steps, this was the access point up into the Cobblers' workshops.

Looking through the archway from the Market Square is Hawkshead's Co-Operative Shop on the right and on the left facing is Tyson's shoe shop in late 1800s Note the cobbles and boy with handcart   *John West*

'Bend or Bump' and the Beatrix Potter Gallery and Ticket Office

Returning once again to the Main Street next to the Post Office, on the left is another National Trust property known as 'Bend or Bump'. This is a fairly modern name for the building, as old locals have pointed out, it would appear that it acquired this name sometime in the 1920s.

The building is difficult to date, it could be early 18th century or even late 17th century. When looking inside most of the interior woodwork seems to point to those dates, with the exception of one interior panelled wall, though this could be fake. 'Bend or Bump' was not a free standing building, it was actually built to fill a gap between two other buildings. One of these was one of the aforementioned Noble'

Cottages and the other what is now the Beatrix Potter Gallery. The earliest mention that I have come across appears in 1743 when it was owned by a Mr Joseph Keen.

According to Parish Accounts (Records) he was 'jack of all trades', as he was described as a carpenter, blacksmith, cordwainer (shoemaker) and an innkeeper. He was innkeeper at the Tanners Arms in 1746 but by then he had left 'Bend or Bump' and it is presumed that he had earlier used part of 'Bend or Bump' as an ale house. This is more than likely possible but not proven. Besides being used as an ale house, the building has had many uses - grocer's, butcher's and slaughterhouse, saddler's shop, shoemaker's, confectioner's and also became Hawkshead Police Station. It must be pointed out that not all these businesses were in the house itself, some if not most, were in the section which juts out into the road on the left, that which is today the Beatrix Potter Gallery Ticket Office. The last individual owner of the building was Beatrix Potter's husband, Mr W D Heelis, who willed the property to the National Trust in 1947.

W D HEELIS ('Appleby Willie') Attorney's Office

The main business property of W D Heelis, known locally as 'Appleby Willie' (derives Appleby from where he was born and his first name was William), was actually next door in what is now the Beatrix Potter Gallery. At first the building was leased by his uncle, William Hopes Heelis in 1861, as a partner of John Slater another Hawkshead attorney. On John Slater's death, he bought the property in 1867 and eventually it passed on to 'Appleby Willie' and on his death in 1947, as already mentioned this went to the National Trust.

Beatrix Potter Gallery

Today the Beatrix Potter Gallery is one of the main visitor attractions in the area, attracting thousands of people from all over the world. To the left of the Gallery is an archway which covers the entrance to the Red Lion Yard with the Red Lion Inn being next door. Originally this was a connecting passage between the two buildings.

The Red Lion Inn

The Red Lion itself is a 15th century property and is one of the more interesting inns in the town. Although today it is almost unrecognisable in comparison to the original structure.

The earliest records that I have regarding the Red Lion and its various properties date from 1689 and was known as the Red Lyon Inn. It is thought that originally it was called the 'Pig and Whistle' but I have found no documentary proof of this to date. There are two plaster figures situated underneath the eaves above the front door, which seem to support this theory, but during the 1850s-60s this property and the adjoining building, the Gallery, had their frontages completely altered and rebuilt by the then innkeeper, Mr Ferdinando Taylor, who by trade was also an architect.

The most prosperous time for the Red Lion appears to be between the early part of the 18th up to the middle part of the 19th centuries. In 1800 the Red Lion was bought by Mr Edward Coward for the sum of £601, with the following land and rights:-

"Two barns, a stable, a cow house, hayloft, cart house, the New Barn, sink pump, a pew in church (northwest gallery in the corner), Dixon Moss and two further peat mosses at Field Head, a peat moss at High Cragg Intake and one at High Moor, one pasture field called, The Park and lastly two dwelling houses in the Red Lion Yard, rented to Mr Thomas Burton and Mr Michael Briggs."

Also mentioned and described is an extension to the north of the main building, rented by a Mr Thomas Robinson, (described in the Parish Registers as a weaver), complete with its own privy and dunghill stead.

This northern extension is worth having a separate mention. It was actually part of the original building and could give us a clue as to what the frontage of the main building looked like, prior to the main alterations. The large gable end of today's building was in reality an internal supporting wall and from here the property extended northwards some thirty feet. It was built on the early style with two shop areas downstairs, set back in from the road and with a large jetted frontage above. The extension was pulled down in 1814 for unknown reasons but it was definitely in use up until that date as the last occupant was Mr Robert Noble, a town shoemaker, who then moved into the Market Square.

Again in 1854, the Red Lion empire was further enlarged, Mr Taylor purchased three more fields, Hewan (or Edwyn's) Meadow, Long Meadow and Hodgson Meadow for the sum of £104, from Mr Edmund Hodgson, of Glenhouse, Hobart Town, Van Deimans Land (Australia).

Coach and four outside the Red Lion 1910-12
(Dick Kirk standing on left with his dog and the ostler is Mr Tinkler (in waistcoat helping gentleman down)

Points of interest - Signatures on window pane

One of the curiosities concerning the Red Lion was a window pane, on which Mr William Wilberforce (famous anti-slavery campaigner who died in 1833), had scratched his signature but sadly, this window pane has disappeared.

In an abstract of title dated 1876 it shows that Mr Taylor also had recourse to rent extra land.

"A common garden at the Croft, at £1.8.0d per year.

Several parcels of land at Hannikin Syke, at £2.9.4d per year.

A further peat moss at Field Head at 4/- per year.

A house at Thompson Ground at 12/- per year.

And a piece of land at Keen Ground at £2.7.3 halfpence per year."

But something seriously must have gone wrong, for in late 1876 all the property was sold to Mr William Francis Barrow (by trade a blacksmith and wheelwright), for the sum of £1,400. Mr Taylor had originally purchased the property in 1853 and paid £2,549.

Smuggling

During the earlier part of the 19th century the Red Lion had another use. The room that is now the 'snug', on the right as you enter by the front door, was used by H.M's Excise Officers and also combined as a Post Office. There are four mentions of this that I have been able to find. Firstly, between 1794 and 1799 whilst Thomas Garnett was landlord, it states in Barfoot and Wilkes Universal British Directory, that the Red Lion whilst also an inn, was classed as a Post Office and Excise House, with a Mr John Aneley as resident Excise Officer. Then from 1828 to 1834 Mr James Dowbiggin occupied the position, along with Mr William Mattinson. But by 1848 Mr Abraham Southward had taken over as Hawkshead's Excise Officer, an unusual coincidence arises here, on the same side of the building as the snug but upstairs in the top room at the back, there is a priest hole, which is where our intrepid local smugglers would hide! It is interesting to note, that although it is in the same building, there is no indication that anyone was actually caught. Most of the smuggling in this area was of the home-brewed variety, mainly whisky. One of our famous exponents of the art was Mr Lancelot Slee, or 'Lanty Slee' as he was locally known and he came from Langdale. In all, he had over twenty-seven stills working for him but not all at the same time. Two of these were within a mile of Hawkshead itself. There are many tales about Lanty Slee's exploits!

RED LION YARD TO HAWKSHEAD POLICE STATION

Red Lion Yard - Victory Cottage

The cobbled road behind and to the right of the Red Lion is called the Red Lion Yard. Most of the buildings here were once part of the Red Lion properties. Those on the left (now private houses) were used as stabling areas. Victory Cottage at the bottom on the left is quite interesting. If you look at the main house wall you can see where it has been altered and extended over many years. An unusual tale is attached to this particular building. Some time in the late 1800s the building, long before it was used as a dwelling house, had been leased out to a local snigging firm ('snigging' is the term used to describe the extraction of felled timber by horses), the company owner had got himself into severe financial difficulties. Most of the work over a period of years, had been carried out in very marshy ground causing him to lose many animals to foot rot. He hit on rather an ingenious idea. Back then throughout the country, many of our landed gentry were creating private zoological gardens, from one of which he managed to acquire a camel. Now, unlike a horse's hoof a camel's hoof is designed to spread its weight in sand instead of sinking. This also seemed to work just as well in marshy ground. Eventually, through the introduction of the camel, he managed to get his business back in the black! Better than that, he made even more money by renting the camel out to other snigging teams in the area and to the same ones that had scoffed at him when he first told them of his idea!

New Barn or 'The Hanging Barn'

The barn on the right, facing Victory Cottage at the bottom of the yard is the 'New Barn' mentioned earlier. It also had another name, somewhat more gruesome, 'The Hanging Barn'. The building through the gap to the right is our old abattoir or butching house and is now converted to a private dwelling. Before the animals were slaughtered they were taken into the Hanging Barn and tied by the neck to rings in the wall. They were starved of food and drink for two to three days, so that when they were eventually slaughtered there was far less mess than normal.

Last Blacksmith's shop (now Doctor's Surgery)

Behind the New Barn we find our present Doctor's Surgery, which moved here from the Red Lion Square in 1995. Prior to being the Surgery it was a private house, which had been converted from Hawkshead's last blacksmith's shop. The original building had consisted of the smithy downstairs at the front and just behind at the back a butcher's shop, owned by the Warriner family. Upstairs from front to back was a large hayloft with access gained by a flight of stone flag steps.

Today the Red Lion Yard finishes here but before our bypass was built (the North Lonsdale Road) the roadway carried on down towards Black Beck Lodge. The uneven road, starting at the corner of Anvil Cottage and leading past the right-hand side of the Red Lion up towards Main Street, is a private road. It once belonged to the Red Lion but now is owned by the owners of Victory Cottage, who are descendants of Mr John Carradus, a former Red Lion innkeeper, from the turn of the century.

We will now make our way towards Black Beck Lodge. Please take care when crossing the North Lonsdale Road. Take the pathway round to the right, in the bottom on the left is the Lodge itself.

Old smithy, Red Lion Yard -1890. Standing on the left holding the horse is presumably the owner of horse, in the middle shoeing the horse is the smithy owner, Thomas Satterthwaite and his helper on the right, Thomas Shepherd.

Black Beck Lodge (Dye House)

The exact age of the building is difficult to determine as it has been added to many times but early to mid 17th century could be about right. Although the first mention of it that I have come across is 1776 when it was known as the Dye House. There is a strong possibility of a connection with Hawkshead's wool trade. It was then owned by a Mr William Jackson of Holme Ground who had sold it to a Mr James Alexander of Keen Ground. At that time it was described as consisting of a dwelling house and one or two outhouses. The field directly behind the building is the aforementioned Hewan Meadow and running through it towards the Lodge is a watercourse made of stone flags. But in the 1950s there was also found the remains of an older watercourse made in an older and more traditional design out of oak shelvings. It was not complete but ran along, in part, in the direction of the flag watercourse of today. But even this is old and must date back well over one hundred and fifty years. There are said to be at least two wells on the property but it is unsure that this watercourse actually feeds them, as an older one runs down the Red Lion Yard towards the Lodge from the town.

By the turn of the 19th century the name Dye House was obsolete, it was now called the Lodge. I will not bother to list all the tenants and owners here but a quick mention of one or two is worthwhile. Mr Taylor, the Red Lion innkeeper, at one time also owned the Lodge and it would appear that both properties were often mortgaged by him. This could account for the financial loss on the sale of the Red Lion Inn. From the Census Returns it shows him living there in 1841 and employing two journeymen plasterers and two apprentices. It was mentioned earlier that his main trade was architect, so his business may have been quite large.

Another owner of the property was Beatrix Potter. She purchased it in 1943 along with others shortly before she died. It was willed to the National Trust a year later in 1944.

To the left of the Lodge is a small cottage, which is today separate from the main building but still owned by the National Trust. This is a converted barn. The earliest mention of the barn is in 1807, where it is described as 'partly built'.

Gallowbarrow

Turning back to the North Lonsdale Road, taking care whilst crossing over, bear right along the footpath keeping the residents' car park on the left, we arrive back on Main Street. Here we will pause and look to our right. The hill in front of you is known as Gallowbarrow, the site of one of Hawkshead's three known gallows or public hanging trees.

The main road leaving Hawkshead over Gallowbarrow, takes you on to Coniston and Ambleside and is flanked by two residential areas. On the left is Hawksgarth, a council estate built around the 1930s and on the right is private housing some of which are relatively modern.

Greenbank Hotel

To the left heading back into town is Hawkshead Garage/petrol station built in 1933 by Mr J M Coward with the Greenbank Hotel to its right. The original house is now split up into two properties with a third more modern house built within the grounds. Greenbank only became a hotel/guest house during the 1960s when it was owned by a Captain Fox. Prior to that its use had been that of gentleman's residence. The exact age of the main buildings is unknown but in a sketch from the early 1800s it is shown as a farm complete with a spinning gallery running along its right-hand gable wall. It was about this time that the farm must have been finished, as an early record dated 1821 states that it was owned as a private residence by a Mr Samuel Clarke (gent) and his wife, Dorothy.

Now we will turn around and head off back into Hawkshead town.

Hawkshead Police Station, Police Houses and Court House

The large building on the left-hand side of the road is Hawkshead Police Station, which was built in 1883 by the Lancashire Constabulary. This not only housed our Police Sergeant and Police Constable but also provided the town with its first purpose-built court room. The court room has long ago been disused and part of its interior furniture now adorns a public bar in Bowness-on-Windermere. Alas, Hawkshead Police Station closed in 1999 as a result of budget restraints and converted into flats.

Justice meeted out over the years

Over many centuries various buildings in Hawkshead have been used as 'Justice Rooms'. The first was at Hawkshead Hall where today we have the remains of our monastery. Here the Cistercian Monks of Furness held sway (power), meeting out their own brand of justice. The road leading out of Hawkshead over the hill towards Ambleside as mentioned previously is known as Gallowbarrow and is said to be the site of the Monastic Gallows. Other places used in the town were the main Assembly

Hawkshead Police Station and Magistrates Court early 1900s

Rooms in the Market House (after the 1790 rebuild) and also peculiarly enough, the top floor at the rear of the Red Lion Inn.

Point of interest - 'Mock' or 'Kangaroo Court' - Outgate Inn

There was also one other court held in the area and that was at Outgate, just to the north of Hawkshead. Rather a strange one but worth a mention here. It was basically a mock (kangaroo!) court held there in the 19th century and could well have been the remains of a much older local custom. This court was held to deal out punishments for minor offences such as drunkenness and awarded small penalties and fines. More a comic opera than a court, the main dignitaries were: the bishop, the justice, the parson and Lord Short of Birkwray and was probably held at Outgate Inn.

The antiquity of this mock court is uncertain but it could indeed be quite old. An entry in the Parish Register among the burials of 1699 may well be a clue to its age: "ffebruary XVIJth Jo Rigg Lord"

WANSFELL VIEW, MAIN STREET TO LEATHER, RAG AND PUTTY STREET

Main Street - Wansfell View

We will now turn our attention to the other side of the street, dealing with it as a whole, from Gilmarva House, the grey building opposite the Red Lion Inn, down as far as Wansfell View at the northernmost end of the street. Starting with Wansfell View, this building was originally the farm carpenter's workshop, with adjoining timber storage shed. The storage shed was on the right where today can be seen two large bay windows. This part of the building was added as an extension but the date is unknown. The main body of the building comprised downstairs, the carpenter's workshop which ran front to back, with the back door leading straight out into open fields. (Today the two fields, Back o' Barn and Bowling Green, have almost disappeared underneath a modern housing estate). The main entrance to the workshop was at the front of the building. Where the larger window is today, there were two large oak doors. Just inside on the left there was a well but this has long since been filled in and covered up. Upstairs was apprentice's accommodation.

Holme Lea and Barn Syke

Next door to Wansfell View are two more cottages, Holme Lea and Barn Syke. Originally these cottages formed one building, downstairs was a long stable or shippon (cow shed) area, whilst upstairs was used as a large hayloft. Looking up at the front of these cottages, three windows can be seen but looking around the rear on both cottages the central windows are at least two feet deeper. At one time, flights of stone flag steps led up to these, as originally they were used as hayloft doors.

Ivy House Hotel

Adjoining Barn Syke on the left (syke is the local term for side) stands an annex of the Ivy House Hotel. This was formerly a stable area, barn and hayloft, with a loft door on the front gable facing the street but this was without a stairway access. Today the building has been much altered. Originally the downstairs side (going up the driveway) was open fronted, whilst above the hayloft had a pegged or slated wall. The driveway itself originally bore round to the left, behind what is now the hotel building and into the farmyard beyond.

Ivy House is of typical late Georgian design, built sometime between 1805 and the late 1820s, definitely later than 1805, as a landscape painting of the northern end of Hawkshead of that year (now in the Abbot Hall Gallery in Kendal), shows clearly a barn on the site of what is now the Ivy House Hotel front garden. The property derived its name from the fact that the building was originally covered across the front and right-hand gable with ivy.

Old Cobblers Tea Shop

To the left of the Ivy House Hotel we find the 'Old Cobblers Tea Shop', a small family run café. This building which still belongs to Gilmarva House next door, was the old farmstead. The tea shop gets its name from Hawkshead's last town cobbler, Mr Charlie 'Clogger' Brown. The tea shop was his workplace and shoe shop. Mr Brown, incidentally, used to make and repair clogs belonging to Beatrix Potter but she would only ever give him one to repair at a time. Just one of her many eccentricities. The property, including Gilmarva House, was bought by Mr Brown at a public sale in 1932. This property, along with nineteen other properties and field lots, were sold by the executors of Mrs Elizabeth Lane who had died in 1919. The Lane family were one of the principal landowners in the area at that time, her husband had been one of our three town doctors, living at Roger Ground just outside Hawkshead. Whilst in their possession, the tea shop part of the property had been leased out to other local businesses. Prior to Mr Brown, was Mr William Bolton, one of the town's painter and decorators as well as photographer. He used the front part as a paint shop and general store, with access around the back into what is now called 'Wordsworth Street'.

Mr Bolton was noted for two things in Hawkshead: one was the shop's front door, it was said to be multi-coloured, evidently before cleaning his paint brushes he would wipe off the excess paint on his front door. The other item is regarding the church. It was he who after being tasked with redecorating the church in 1875, discovered previously unknown murals above the arches, within the church itself. He was then given the honour of touching up the murals, as they can be seen today.

William Bolton - painter, decorator and photographer (standing with his pipe on far right), sitting is Thomas S Bradley and on his left is Harry S Bolton ('The New Stores' in the Square, changed to Coffee Pot and now Whigs Café) and Harry's wife in the doorway.

John West

Wordsworth Street originally Ann or Queen Anne Street
(Known locally as 'Leather, Rag and Putty Street')

Again leaving Main Street, turn right up the second of Hawkshead's few remaining cobbled streets. Today this is known as Wordsworth Street, mainly through tourism and Anne Tyson's Cottage. A fairly modern name for a very old street. Originally as far as I can ascertain, it was known as Ann or Queen Anne Street, more than likely the latter. The former being more folklorist, with the cottage belonging to Ann Tyson.

The locals however have their own name for this particular street and that is, 'Leather, Rag and Putty Street'. It got its name from some of the different trades carried out there over many, many years. On the left, the frontages of these buildings (facing the Red Lion Square and on up to the archway), were essentially connected with the rag trade, draper's, milliner's, seamstress and a tailor's shop. The last tailor there was a Mr Tyson who owned the buildings directly opposite the Co-Operative. Mr Tyson when he packed up his business actually became a Co-Operative manager at the then new Ambleside branch. To finish off the rag trade, there was also a draper's shop at the top of the street on the right-hand side. The very first mention of a draper's shop, would be the one owned by Ann Tyson in the late 1700s.

The putty came from the painting and decorating profession. There was one established business at the top of the steps to the left, where today's 'Tigers Eye Gem Stone Jewellery Shop' is situated, with Mr William Bolton's business on the other side of the street, where today can be seen a pale green door (previously multi-coloured

Leather, Rag and Putty Street in early 1900s. On the right is Gilmarva House and note the steps leading up to leather workers workshop.

from cleaning his brushes!).

The leather part of the name came from the leather industry which, after the wool trade started to die out, became a major employer in the area. The building on the right, which sticks out into the street, was the main leather property here. Today the building is a holiday cottage but a hundred years ago looked quite different. Where today can be seen a balcony area, here was a flight of stone and flag steps leading up into a leather worker's workshop. The modern garage area on the right was knocked through some thirty years ago or more. The original building had been built up on stilts, with two tan pits underneath. The property as a whole was called a tannery. There were one or two in the town and many others in the outlying farmsteads. Although the latter were run mainly as an extra source of income for the farmers and not as professional tanning businesses.

Further up the street, on the left, is another flight of stone and flag steps. These led up to the last cobbler's workshop on Leather, Rag and Putty Street, which was owned by a Mr Fred Coward. Before he moved to these premises he had one of the cobbler's workshops above the Co-Operative. The property on the opposite side of the street is today part of a Bed and Breakfast establishment which incorporates the original Ann Tyson's cottage.

At the top of the right-hand side of these buildings, next to the old tannery, used to stand another cobbler's workshop belonging to the Coward family. In fact even today all the property on the right of the street and around the corner, up to and including Ann Tyson's Cottage, is still in the hands of the Coward family and has been for well over a hundred years.

There have, of course, been many other businesses on this street over the years but the ones mentioned here, were mainly instrumental with the name 'Leather, Rag and Putty'. Whilst walking up the street you will have noticed the two ruts on either side. These have been caused by the passage of countless horses and carts over many years. It is interesting to note that the first mention of four-wheeled transport in Hawkshead was as late as 1792, when in the Parish Accounts (Records) a 'chaise driver' is mentioned. This however cannot be taken as a hard and fast date, it would have been much earlier.

Grandy Nook to Flag Street

Grandy Nook

Arriving at the top of Leather, Rag and Putty Street, we come to a small junction in the road. This, or to be more accurate, the archway on the left, is known as 'Grandy Nook'. The tarmac road leading underneath the archway leads into the Red Lion Square and from the archway going backwards up the hill, is today called Vicarage Lane. This lane is formed from part of one of the old packhorse routes into the town and led here from the Furness peninsular.

The archway itself could well date from the 15th century or earlier and as one local tale suggests, used by Hawkshead's fighting men as a means of crossing the street without being seen by the enemy (possibly the Scottish Border Reivers). Grandy Nook gets its name from the old English and local dialect - 'grandy' being grandmother and 'nook' being corner. Grandmother's corner thus suggests a strong link with the woollen industry. It is quite easy to imagine the old dames of the town gathering here to spin and weave, passing the time of day chattering and gossiping. Many's the tale this quaint corner could tell!

Grandy Nook Tea Rooms

Standing with your back to the Grandy Nook archway, facing you is today's Grandy Nook Tea Rooms. This property takes its name from the archway opposite and was originally named by a past owner. This building was built in 1668 on the site of one

Grandy Nook on the right (looking through is the Co-Operative shop) and Wordsworth Street (known locally as Leather, Rag and Putty Street) on the left (note the ash cart) in 1916.

of Hawkshead's last thatched cottages. Not thatched as they do down south but using bracken and ling. (Ling is a form of heather). This property like several others in the town, was used at one stage as a small local school, separate from the Grammar School. One of the teachers known to have used this building was a Mr John Harrison, who seemed to be quite an influence on the young William Wordsworth. Although Mr Harrison would by then have been an old man.

T W Thompson, author of 'Wordsworth's Hawkshead' (edited by Mr Robert Woof), who lived here during the mid part of the last century (1944 to mid 1950s), thought that at one time it could have been an alehouse. I recently came across an article in Barrow Records Office, which states that during the 1790s, Mr Miles Robinson, victualler and carpenter lived there and it was known as the 'Carpenters Arms'. According to T W Thompson the property had been bought by Myles Robinson, house carpenter in April 1771 for the sum of £131. 5s. 0d, from the Reverend Thomas Deason.

Ann Tyson's Cottage

Just around the corner to the left, we find Ann Tyson's cottage. This is where the young William Wordsworth and his elder brother Richard first lodged as children whilst attending Hawkshead Grammar School. The subject of Wordworth's school life in Hawkshead has been dealt with before by many people many times, so here I intend to dwell only briefly on the subject in connection with his lodgings.

The cottage could well date back to the mid 15th or early 16th century. When Ann and her husband Hugh Tyson lived there, it was known as Green End Cottage, and it got this name because it was the nearest dwelling house to Hawkshead's first bowling green. I mentioned earlier the two fields that used to be behind Wansfell View on Main Street. This is where the one called Bowling Green got its name and it borders the side and rear of Ann Tyson's Cottage.

It would appear that the first children to attend the Grammar School were automatically found accommodation in the Masters' Lodgings, the Old Schoolhouse, at Hickey Turnings where we started our tour. Anyone arriving late had to find their own lodgings in the town. This is where the Wordsworth boys came. Ann Tyson was one of many dames in the area who took in the young lodgers as an extra source of income. Both Ann and Hugh had their own businesses. Hugh was a carpenter by trade and Ann ran a small draper's shop. The Wordsworth boys' rooms were upstairs on the right. The main upper right-hand window is said to have been their study and it was here that the young William carved his name on the inside window-seat. Richard his brother, also carved his name but in a window to the rear of the building. Unfortunately during the 1870s a local carpenter from Hannikin was tasked with doing some work inside and he inadvertently removed William's carving but at least two copies were known to have been made. On various parts of the property, appear other carvings made by other young lodgers who were known to have stayed with Ann Tyson at the same time as the Wordsworth boys, thus helping to prove that young William did in fact lodge here.

The reason that I added the last sentence, is that over the years the argument has arisen over the exact whereabouts of Wordsworth's lodgings. For shortly after the Wordsworth boys arrived, Ann and Hugh moved out of Hawkshead town, across the valley to the hamlet of Colthouse. As you enter Colthouse on the left is a large property known as Green End. Behind this building on the other side of Scarhouse Lane, is another Green End Cottage and this is where the Tysons moved to but there is also proof that the Wordsworth boys lodged at this site. For young William described two views of a wood, one from the front door step and one from an upstairs window. He was describing Spring Wood behind Colthouse which could not have been seen from Ann Tyson's Cottage in Hawkshead. One small point I would like to add is this: Wordsworth also describes a 'boxed in stream' and this particular phrase has in the past been used as proof of Wordsworth's stay at Colthouse. Back then, most if not all the becks and streams in and around the town were lined with stone flags, hence 'boxed in'! Even today if you look carefully, examples of these can still readily be found.

Anyhow enough of the Colthouse connection, back to Ann Tyson's Cottage. Although the property is used today as a Bed and Breakfast establishment, the interior of the building has changed little but the exterior has altered somewhat. Starting with the right-hand gable, here up until about 1905 was the remains of one of Hawkshead's many spinning galleries. When the woollen trade had died out in Hawkshead many of the galleries, both spinning and drying, were removed. In some cases these galleries were covered in with a pegged wall (slated) and used as extensions to the upper floors, as was the one here. There are only two of these galleries left in Hawkshead today and these I will point out shortly.

The area in front of the cottage at one time was one of Hawkshead's many public squares but around the turn of the century it was walled off and claimed as a private garden for the cottage. These small, open areas were deliberately left as public ground to provide ample turning space for the horses and carts, allowing easier access through the narrow streets. The chimney on the right at the front of the building has lost a section in height and the central window upstairs at the front, one of the original 17th century ones, has been replaced with a more modern one. Two other windows have been added over the years, one at the front at the top of the steps and one upstairs on the left-hand extension. The extension itself is old and up until 1863 was Hawkshead's first Methodist Chapel. The wooden banisters which ran up the side of the steps have been removed and attached to the steps at the front, a modern balcony has been added, although tastefully done, in local stone. Downstairs, underneath the left-hand extension, was a stable and shippon area, these are as untouched today as when they were first built. This may well have been Hugh Tyson's carpenter's workshop.

There is a gap between the gable of the left-hand extension and the small shed next door but originally there was a building standing here. Unfortunately there is only one old sketch available of this missing building and it is very difficult to glean any useful information from it. At first glance the small shed on the left appears to be half a building and this is more than probable. The front and left-hand wall are made from stone flags (which I shall come back to shortly) but the right-hand wall is made from local stone. It is known that the missing building's walls were also made from flags so instead of having two properties it is more than likely to have been one complete building. Probably through neglect one half was taken down and a newer dry stone wall was added to the half in better condition, so it could be retained as a shed. The flag walls that I mentioned earlier are unique to this area and were a much easier way of walling properties. The older dwelling houses in the town could well have been built using this method of construction. Firstly a timber framework would have been built and a ditch dug running along the outside. The flags were then placed into the bottom of the ditch and pushed up towards the timber framework and fastened to it with iron pins. The interior walls would then have been plastered with mud or even animal dung. On this small shed the flag walls can clearly be seen but a better example is the Beatrix Potter Gallery Ticket Office. These two buildings are the best examples in the town today but at one time there were many others. Occasionally we shall come across other stone flags on our route that are much larger than these. When you consider that these flags were taken from the rock manually and that they would have to be dragged from our nearest flag quarries on Borwick Ground Fell some three miles away, it is no mean achievement. To give you an idea as to their length, only two-thirds of the flags are visible above the ground and these are of varying heights.

The wall at the front is known as a 'pegged wall'. It gets this name, not from the method of attaching the slates but from the slate itself. Some of the local quarrying terms for the different grades are London, Duchess, Tom and Pegg. Pegg is a lower grade of roofing slate and these were attached to the walls as a defence against the rain, to which they are ideally suited but no good at all against draught. These people of yesteryear were not daft, they packed in behind the slates with moss. Now, if you take a selection of all the different mosses that grow in the area and dry them out until they are tinder dry, then put a match to them they will all flare up, except one, which is sphagnum moss. It goes bright red and goes out. So they may have used it not just as draught-proofing but possibly as a protection against fire.

Wordsworth's Lodgings 1880s (Ann Tyson's Cottage). Note the steps leading up to first Methodist Chapel

Looking up the lane on the left, a modern extension can be seen with a high stone wall running off it and a small passage or 'weint' (pronounced 'went') at the top side. Back in the 1700s this formed half of a large orchard belonging to Mr Edward Satterthwaite. Inadvertently, the property and land owned by this gentleman is most important to a central part of the town's history and local development.

Before I explain this, we shall carry on up the lane as far as the white cottages on the left.

Little Force Cottage and Greenhow Cottages

All these white cottages are today owned by the National Trust, kindly donated by Mrs Bertha Peacock. The topmost cottage is known as Little Force Cottage and was at first a farmhouse, with a farmyard behind it. The dating of this building is awkward because of the necessary replacement work carried out on the property, I would suggest mid 18th century but it could be earlier. The two cottages just below are known as Greenhow Cottages. You could at a glance date these buildings at around 1719 because of a spice cupboard to be found inside, personally I am not too sure, as I think that the spice cupboard was a later addition from another building. There are one or two pointers to my theory.

'Wee Cottage'

Firstly, let us assume that Little Force Cottage was a farmhouse with a small barn attached to its top end. As a farmhouse it was quite large and it could be presumed that it would have one or two farm buildings close by. Greenhow Cottages appear to be what they were called. It seems strange that they would build two cottages with

Vicarage Lane covered in heavy snow in 1930s. On the immediate right is Jasmine Cottage and The Cottage, looking down the lane towards Ann Tyson's Cottage

such an unusually high right-hand gable. Now, between this odd high gable and the left-hand gable of the old farmhouse can be found 'Wee Cottage'. What you see is what you get, this is a suspended building. It is known that the pantry in 'Wee Cottage' is in fact a blocked off door but surely not into the attic of Greenhow Cottages, this does not seem to make sense. It is however more probable, that a barn stood on this site before the cottages and they were built at a later date. This would mean that the access to 'Wee Cottage' was much easier and that the entry underneath 'Wee Cottage' was designed as a cart track giving access to the farmyard behind. When the barn was pulled down the original doorway to 'Wee Cottage' was closed up and moved round to the front where it is today, complete with a set of stone flag steps.

Flag Cottage (old spelling 'Flagg')

To shed further light on my as yet admittedly unproved theory - in 1777 there were five cottages built on part of Edward Satterthwaite's garden/orchard. Three of these remain; Jasmine Cottage, The Cottage and further down through the alleyway on the right is Flag Cottage. The alleyway is not the original one, this right of way used to run through Edward Satterthwaite's garden/orchard and was known as the 'ancient usuall and occupational way'. Noticing the slightly raised flag step and wooden door at this disused right of way, (which still has its original cobbled floor), take a walk through the present alleyway into the top end of Flag Street.

Directly ahead of us, 'from the photograph' (top of Flag Street) you can see Flag Cottage, the fourth cottage stretched out from Flag Cottage as far as the town beck and as you see from the photograph it had its chimney stack on the left-hand gable. This building was pulled down in 1929 and the ground that it had occupied was turned into the present garden area that you see today. Although then the garden (up until 1998) rose up at an angle to the top of the wall at the back. When it was cleared there was exposed the rear wall, which clearly showed another chimney stack, this belonged to the fifth property, which had to go back into what is now the gardens of Greenhow Cottages.

Back in the 1700s the area where we are standing was not cobbled or flagged but was of hard-packed earth and led down towards the town beck. At that time the beck flowing through the town was wide open and because these new built cottages had no sewage systems, it ran through the town as an open sewer. In saying that, it was also being used as a public thoroughfare at the same time. The present garden area on the left, looking down the street would have sloped down towards the beck bottom with a possible walkway for pedestrians but if you look at the building on the right, you will see where there is a cut-out section at the bottom of the gable. Normally these are found at a height of between ten and twelve feet above the ground, to allow the passage of a horse and cart. Today it is obviously not high enough but back then when the beck was wide open it would be at the correct height. Further to this, just around the corner is an infilled section of wall, this was an entrance point into what is called Slater's Yard, long ago blocked-up. (We shall visit Slater's Yard shortly). At the other end of this gable is another cut away section but at the correct height. From here the road sloped down round and under into the town beck.

Flag Street

Later on the beck was covered over throughout the town with large stone flags,

Top of Flag Street 1909 (old cottage demolished in 1929 and replaced by a garden)

Flag Street 1890. Note the hole in the street where they entered and went down steps to Vicarage Lane Beck to obtain water. Pegged wall to the left especially in Flag Street, from where it got its name but here they also added a vertical line of flags running up the centre of the street. These were put in so as to provide a safety barrier to allow pedestrians access over the then partially closed-in beck. If you stand half-way along Flag Street and look down towards the end where the tarmac reaches the stone paving slabs, here there was left a hole in the ground with a flight of six steps leading down into the bottom of the beck. There are three stories connected to this. You can make up your own mind which you wish to believe, I know which one I would go for. The first one, is that the hole was left to allow access for the local women to draw water to do their laundry - I very much doubt that! The second is to do with the spinning industry - this is fairly possible! In the old days the wool was spun dirty, the fleece was taken from the sheep, carded and spun, without being washed. The skeins were then pegged out in running water to clean off any excess burrs. The third story is more than likely correct. When they covered the beck up through the town, they had nothing at the top to stop rubbish and debris from flowing down and blocking up beneath the town centre. If this had happened, the water would have backed-up to the top of Flag Street and risen up flooding the houses on the left and right. As you can see today there is no hole in the ground but at the end of January 1995 we had another flood and the depth of the water at the bottom of Flag Street, was up to the author's knees at 6 o'clock in the morning. Once again it shows that these earlier locals were not daft, they had a reason for doing everything. In the early 1980s there was another flood but this was a bad one, the force of the water ripped two huge ruts, three feet deep right through the town. Floods in Hawkshead have been quite common over the years. The earliest mention is from the Parish Registers dated 1686 and reads as follows:-

"Bee it remembered that upon the tenth day of June att nighte in the yeare of our Lord the one thousand sixxe hundred eighty and sixxe there was such a fearefull thunder with fyre and rayne which occasioned such a terrible flood as the like of it was never seene in these parts by noe man livinge; for it did throwe downe some houses and milles and took away seuerall briggs; yea the water did run through houses and did much hurte to houses; besydes the water wash't upp great trees by the roots and the becks and gills carried them with other greate trees stocks and greate stones a greate way off and layed them on mens ground; yea further the water did soe fiercely run down the hyeways and made such deepe holes and ditches in them that att seurall places neither horse nor foote coulde passe; and besydes the becks and rivers did so breake out of their races as they broughte exeedinge great sand beds into mens ground att many places which did greate hurte the neuer like was knowne; I pray God of his greate mercy graunte that none which is now livenge can never see the like againe".

Don't we all!

Walker Ground looking down to the top of Vicarage Lane - roadway torn and broken in early 1980s flood

BERKLEY SQUARE AREA (OLD SPELLING BERKELEY)

Minstrels' Gallery

Having walked down Flag Street we now find ourselves in Berkley Square, one of a few remaining of our several open spaces in the town. It is one of the prettiest corners of Hawkshead but unlike its more famous namesake in London, we have no singing nightingales, just one or two raucous crows! The main building on Berkley Square is the Minstrels' Gallery. Today it is used as a tea room but the building dates in the main from the early 15th century and was one of Hawkshead's several inns and alehouses. It was originally called the 'Crown and Mitre', some time long ago (date unknown) it was changed to the Minstrels' Gallery. Indeed upstairs it had its own gallery with stone seats cut into the walls but unfortunately this was removed some years ago. The building has had many uses over the years besides being an inn. At the turn of the century it was owned by a Mrs Armer who used it as a grocer's and sweet shop. Slightly earlier, it was known to be an apothecary's shop but following Mrs Armer, it has been a private house, guest house, a café on numerous occasions, even a Potter's Studio and shop. Apart from what I mentioned earlier, much of the original interior remains and sticking out from the right-hand upstairs gable, nearest the Kings Arms, is the remains of one of our last two spinning galleries, now forming part of an upstairs room.

Methodist Chapel

Tucked away in the corner to the left of the Minstrels' Gallery is our Methodist Chapel, now a church. The original meeting room was at Ann Tyson's Cottage but in 1863 it was removed to here, thanks to the benevolence of Mr William Satterthwaite

Berkley Square 1898. Methodist Chapel with porch and arched window (third building from left), Armer the Grocer's (now Minstrels' Gallery) and end part of the Kings Arms with horse-drawn cart on the right

JP. It came to Mr Satterthwaite's attention that many people were trying to congregate in rather a small cold room. So he decided to give the Methodists the two properties in the corner of Berkley Square and the two on the right-hand side of Flag Street, which had been willed to him by Mr Edward Satterthwaite, to alleviate their problem. The Berkley Square houses were much altered, one and a half being converted into the chapel, the remainder made into two dwelling houses with a communal garden area in behind. The two dwelling houses were given under three conditions. Firstly, that they were to be rented out only to local people. Secondly, that the rent went towards the upkeep of the chapel. Thirdly, that the occupiers of the houses were responsible for the cleaning of the chapel and general maintenance of the chapel garden. These stipulations applied until quite recently.

Market Square

Turning around, we now enter Hawkshead's main Market Square. With the exception of what is now called the Honey Pot, (a small grocer's and delicatessen) most of the buildings here today have changed considerably in the last two hundred years.

We will start our description of these buildings with the one standing on the right at the bottom of Church Hill. Up until recently this building was split into three separate properties. Downstairs on the right was Hawkshead branch of the National Westminster Bank. Before them it was owned by the Midland Bank. Above the old bank premises, now empty, is a small rentable flat and to the left, a rentable dwelling house. The building was built sometime in the early to mid 18th century, on the site of two earlier small tenements but the original building looked a lot different from that of today. The first known occupants were the Stuart family. It is known that John Stuart, who leased the property in the 18th century was a shoemaker, likewise his son William and they made footwear for the Wordsworth boys. By 1837 the Stuarts had moved out and the next occupants were the Hewitsons (related to the author) and they had the property right up until the early 1900s, at least up until 1907 when my orphaned grandfather moved there to live with his aunt, Mrs Hannah Hewitson. Hannah's husband John was a shoemaker by trade, it would seem that this was the family business. John unwisely invested £500 in a South African Railway venture and invariably lost a small fortune. Devastated, he committed suicide in the property by hanging himself from a spiral staircase which connected the upper floor to the shops below.

In 1912 Hannah allowed her niece, Mary Anne Hewitson (author's great-grandmother) to take over the business premises as a confectioner's shop, which she ran up until 1919 when the property was sold. The Hewitsons then went to live in Victoria Street, next to the Queens Head Hotel.

The frontage of the building in the 19th century consisted of the main house on the left, with the front door in the centre and a large downstairs window to the left of that. Downstairs to the right were two shop fronts. The one farthest right was a shoe repair shop with a cellar access door below and the inner shop was used to sell ready made and new shoes. Upstairs the six modern sash windows did not exist, instead there was a small window on the far right of the building and slightly left of that a small bay window. Between this small bay window and the small window on the right, underneath the eaves was a peculiar oval plaque. The plaque was of Irish origin and

Hewitson's shops - 1907. Town Hall on immediate left, then Hewitson's house, their shoe shop in centre and shoe repair shop on the right

appeared in only one other building in the town, a property now called Lantern Cottage, just behind, in the street next door. Above the front door of the building was a much larger bay window. This was how the frontage looked in 1885 but by 1907 the plaque had disappeared. Instead two rather small windows had been added underneath the eaves, one either side of the smaller bay window. When the two bays were removed and replaced with the six sash windows is not known but the bays certainly added a bit of style. The front of the building had a low fenced wall running nearly full length. The iron railings were removed during the Second World War, when all metal was needed for the armaments industry.

Town Hall (Market House or Market Shambles)

To the left of the bank building at the southern end of the Market Square is Hawkshead's Town Hall or Market House, a property that has undergone many changes over many years. The original Market House or Shambles as it was once known, was a lot smaller than that of today. From written descriptions it was a semi-timber construction. During the time of the Wordsworth boys in Hawkshead, it was said to be in a fairly dilapidated condition. Towards the far end of the building, near Church Stile, was a large boulder, which was used as a play area by the local children, but more of this boulder shortly. In 1789 it was decided to pull down the Old Shambles and replace it with a more modern stone building which was considerably larger. The original Market Shambles was a two storey building measuring forty-seven feet by eighteen feet but the completed new building measured seventy-eight feet by twenty-four feet at either end, front to back. The central section protruded into the Square by another seventeen inches. Incorporated in the downstairs part of the building were ten arches, seven at the front and three on the left-hand side, with three more inside, opposite those on the left but built into a main supporting wall. This downstairs area, the Shambles, was designed in this way so as to incorporate a Yarn Market, as well as the Butchers' Shambles. At one time there were as many as seven butchers working from here on market day. Built into the wall downstairs at the rear of the Shambles, is a small holding cell for prisoners awaiting the Petty Sessions, which were held directly upstairs in the new Assembly Rooms. Either side of the Assembly Rooms on the upstairs floor, were two lodging suites. Of the one on the right to date, I have not been able to find any information but the first occupant of the left-hand suite, was a Mr George Jackson. The steps to the left of the Market House, leading up to the churchyard, are still today known as 'Jackie Steps' and this is from where they got their name. The steps also allowed access to the lodging suite, with a small walled garden to the rear. The door to the right-hand suite was approached from Church Hill on the right. Each lodging suite measured twenty square feet and one of

Town Hall and Market Square 1900s. With Hewitson's shoe shops in the centre and what is now the Honey Pot on the far right

the provisions with the rental meant that on certain days of the year, when functions were held in the Assembly Rooms, if more space was required the tenants had to relinquish their property for the event.

The large boulder mentioned earlier has its own amusing tale. It was known as 'Nanny's Stean' or the 'Rocking Stean'. Presumably it had been deposited during the last Ice Age and Hawkshead had been built around it over the years. It acquired the name 'Nanny's Stean' (stone pronounced 'stayan') from an old lady of eighty called Nanny Holmes, from nearby Sawrey, who on market days used the boulder as a table to sell her wares. When the planned rebuild of 1790 went ahead, she complained bitterly that her 'stall' was being done away with and that her only means of income would cease. One of the benefactors to the proposed new building was Mr William

(Slatey) Rigge, a rich local slate merchant living at Keen Ground, who asked old Nanny what the pitch was worth to her. She replied, "Six pennies a week!" Which was probably more than twice the actual value! Thinking that because of her advanced age she would not last much longer, he promptly agreed to pay this sum weekly for the rest of her life. By all accounts Nanny had the last laugh, Mr Rigge died before her, whilst she lived on to be ninety-five and the executors of his estate, had to pay her six pennies every week until the day she died. Quite canny, our Nanny!

In 1897 the Market House was again altered. This time the right-hand lodging house was done away with, extending the Assembly Rooms and allowing a staircase to be built inside against the gable wall. The left-hand lodging suite was given a downstairs floor and the complete roof was removed and rebuilt as it is today. The next tenant/caretaker was a Mrs Polly Postlethwaite, who turned her new downstairs room into a café and tea rooms and some but not all of the archways were filled in with stone and finished off with arched windows. Two new doors were added at the front, one at the far right and one slightly left of the centre, where it still is today.

Point of interest - Wool and Leather Trade

There has been a market in Hawkshead since letters patent were granted during the reign of James I. Permission was granted to hold a weekly market on Mondays and two annual fairs, both could last two days. One fair was held on the Feast day of St Matthew and the day following and the other at the Feast of Ascension and the day following. In later years, as well as a Monday weekly market, only during the summer months a Friday market was also held. Unfortunately, the Hawkshead markets fell into decline during the 1800s.

The wool and leather trade in Hawkshead had many ups and downs but it would seem that in its heyday it was a thriving community enterprise. Most families produced their own yarn and garments and sold their extra produce at these markets as well as an abundance of fleeces. Wool badgers or merchants' agents were known to have come to Hawkshead from as far away as Cockermouth and Kendal.

Judging by the number of tanners and shoemakers recorded in and around the township of Hawkshead during the 18th and 19th centuries there must have been a high demand for leather and leather products. Hawkshead has long been remembered for its clog and shoe whangs. This is an old local name for leather laces.

T W Thompson ('Wordsworth's Hawkshead') reproduced an old rhyme he discovered in 1906 which goes:

Hawkshead and Kendal are bound up together
Firstly by wool and lastly by leather
Both live by their trade in fair or foul weather
And pay scanty heed to mighty folks blether.

The above rhyme is said to have been written by Mr Thomas Cowperthwaite an 18th century innkeeper at the Red Lion in Hawkshead. Another take from the old local song (origin unknown) which must have something to do with the decline in the wool industry goes like this:

The farmers' daughters formerly were taught to card and spin,
And by their own industry good husbands they would win;

Polly Postlewthaites Tea Rooms 1900, with Polly sitting outside. Gable end of Town Hall and 'Jackie Steps' on the left

45

But now the cards and spinning wheels are forced to take their chance,
And they've hopped off to boarding schools to learn to sing and dance!

Hawkshead Institute and Laburnham House

Looking left again, we come to Hawkshead's Institute which backs onto the Murray Brothers' Woollen Shop. All the buildings in this block are of fairly modern development, except for the bookshop on the extreme left. Prior to 1846 this part of Hawkshead looked very different. The bookshop building was a large eight bedroomed property known as Laburnham House. It stood by itself separate from any other building with a small passage or 'weint' on the right-hand side, with Laburnham Street on the left. At the front was a small open square, whilst at the rear (on Market Square) stood a small outbuilding. There is only one picture available of the original building and can be dated sometime shortly after 1790 (artist unknown). Back then the roof line was completely different to that of today. The rear wall (Market Square) was actually one of the two gables and instead of having five windows as it does today, it had one large square window high up in the centre. The outbuilding was more of a sloping roofed extension, which comprised of two shops, one a milliner's and the other an early stationer's. At that time the property was owned by the Sutherland family.

'The Tanners Arms' ('Hawkshead Institute' now stands)

Moving to the right (pre 1846) stood a most picturesque property, it comprised of a warehouse and two businesses. The two businesses were downstairs. At the front was 'The Tanners Arms' and around the right-hand side was a shoe shop owned by Mr

Tanners Arms 1820 - no longer here. Copy of an old painting of Tanners Arms   Mr R Fowkes

Robert Noble. The frontage of the building was early in design, with a jetted top floor overhanging the bottom by about six feet. The building was half-timber frame and half of stone. The entire upstairs wall at the front was a pegged wall (with the exception of the windows). The Tanners Arms was set back underneath and was one of Hawkshead's oldest drinking establishments. The last known landlord was Mr Joseph Keen (grandson of Joseph Keen of 'Bend or Bump'). The large room above the inn was used as a boot and shoe warehouse for the town's many cobblers and was looked after by Mr Robert Noble, who owned the shoe shop next door. Mr Noble had moved here when his other premises at the Red Lion was pulled down in 1814.

The right-hand side of the building, like the front had a large pegged wall and formed the right-hand gable. Just behind the main building but set back from the road opposite the Barn Studios, was a small tannery and behind that again, opposite the Brown Cow Cottages was a barn and stable belonging to Graythwaite Hall.

Fire - Hawkshead 1846

The date 1846 was significant to all these properties as it was on the 6th, February 1846 that Hawkshead suffered a large fire. With the exception of the barn and tannery, the remainder of the buildings were severely damaged by the fire, along with the two top cottages on Laburnham Street, now Whigs Café. The Kings Arms and its adjoining archway were also damaged. According to a newspaper report of that date the buildings were destroyed but this is a case of 19th century sensationalism. There is a photograph in the author's possession, which clearly shows the Tanners Arms building complete with its roof and Mr Noble's Shoe Shop sign, still standing. Although it is certain that Laburnham House was completely gutted and that had to be rebuilt as it is today.

Excerpt from Westmorland Gazette 7 February 1846

DESTRUCTIVE FIRE AT HAWKSHEAD

This ancient market town was, on Sunday morning last, visited by the serious calamity of fire. Soon after four o'clock, the destructive element broke out in an outhouse occupied by Richard Noble, connected with a quadrangular set of premises at the north-eastern extremity of the Market Place and raging with unmitigated violence, in a short space of time destroyed an extensive stabling, a small dwelling-house, boot and shoe warehouse, and threatened to carry away the King's Arms public-house. This was about half-past five o'clock and it was then fearfully anticipated that not only the whole of these extensive premises, but a great portion of the town would fall a sacrifice. A violent north wind prevailed, which added to the fury of the flames. If we could have divested ourselves of a feeling of sympathy for human suffering, and stood indifferent spectators, to the situation of wretched neighbours in a state of nudity, we might indeed have said the scene was awfully grand. A large body of inhabitants had soon assembled (expresses having been sent in all directions for help) who used every exertion to extinguish the flames, and they were encouraged by several gentlemen who were actively engaged in assisting the sufferers to remove their property to a place of safety. Fortunately, at the hour just mentioned, the extreme violence of the wind abated; about five minutes afterwards it again rose but as it blew now from the west the flames were driven back from the path of destruction. There was a partial re-commencement beyond the place where the fire originated, and two dwelling houses sustained much damage, but as all efforts were turned in this direction, the two contiguous dwellings occupied by Mrs Bragg and Robert Stoddard, were saved. This dreadful fire lasted upwards of three hours before the danger entirely ceased. Its origin purely accidental. We understand the owners of the property, Mr B Hawkrigg, the Misses Rowlandson, with the exception of Mr Slater, are fully insured, but we are glad to state that the loss sustained by the latter gentleman is inconsiderable. The heaviest sufferer is Mr Robert Noble, whose stock was heavy and valuable and the chief part of which is destroyed, but his papers and books were saved. Mrs Gill's loss is heavy (King's Arms).

The Tanners Arms building was eventually pulled down in 1892 and the Hawkshead Institute was built in its place, essentially as reading rooms upstairs and the downstairs was used as a tea room. Today downstairs there is a craft and gift shop, whilst the upstairs has been turned into a vegetarian restaurant.

The old tannery and barn had largely escaped the blaze but these two buildings were also altered after the fire. Immediately following the fire, the tannery was converted into a small dwelling house with a spiral staircase leading down into the square, at Church Stile, opposite the Barn Studios. The barn stayed as it was for a while, with a set of stone flag steps leading up to the hayloft above, with a well and pump at the base of the steps.

In 1902 both the dwelling house and barn were pulled down and replaced in 1903, with the building standing there today. This new building upstairs was incorporated with the Institute and was used as a games room, complete with snooker tables and a small library. The downstairs rooms were taken over by a Mrs McGarr, who used it as a sweet shop and tobacconist's. Over the years this downstairs section has had many other uses - Home Guard Station, coal merchant's, garage, printer's shop, butcher's and now a shop selling woollens.

Mrs McGarr and her tobacconist shop 1920s

Kings Arms Hotel (Kings Head)

Walking back into the Market Square at the northern end, we find the Kings Arms Hotel, formerly known as the Kings Head. This building was severely damaged by the fire of 1846. Most of its original frontage disappeared along with the entire top floor, which is why the roofline today is much lower than that of the adjoining archway

The archway too was badly damaged. The wall facing the square, like the one at the rear is still a pegged wall. I have not been able to trace any pictures of the original front of the Kings Arms, so we don't really know what it looked like. As to the age of the building, it is difficult to say, the Kings Arms has been altered many times both in size and shape, both inside and out. However, some clues still remain inside, such as the low roofed ceilings downstairs in what is now the public bar. Most of the oak beams seem to be original, along with the deep set windows on the left-hand gable and rear walls. Some of the interior walls are main supporting walls and give us a clue to the building's original shape and there still remains downstairs, an oak mullioned window. Because of fire damage and the many alterations, recent and not so recent, the upper floor is not much help in dating the property. So all we have are the aforementioned clues. I would suggest that a 15th century building stood on the site, although little remains of it today.

Attached to the front of the building, on the left is a two storey extension made from red brick. This was probably added as an outhouse after the fire of 1846. It is known that during the 1860s, Mr Robert Kirby the then landlord, used this extension to house his prize trail hound. Evidently Mr Kirby followed the hound trails with great enthusiasm and purchased the dog on good faith as a 'sure fire winner'. By all accounts it wasn't cheap and he laid out quite a sum of money. Shortly after buying the dog, there was a hound trail to be held locally and thinking that no-one around knew the dog's pedigree and form, he entered the dog and placed a substantial amount of money on it to win. Even though a few close friends in the trailing community advised against it, he was so cocksure that he was going to make a packet,

Kings Arms Hotel 1920s - on right, (Mr Milner was licensee). On the left is Esthwaite Café (Honey Pot), Methodist Chapel and what is now Minstrels' Gallery

he ignored their advice and went ahead. Sure enough, from the start the dog led the field racing away across the meadows, the main pack being left behind, when all of a sudden it spotted a rabbit and left the trail in pursuit of its prey - the race forgotten! Two days later, this thoroughbred amongst trail hounds, turned up in the bar of the Kings Arms. Mr Kirby promptly grabbed it, took it away to the outhouse and hung it by the neck from the rafters. Whether it caught the rabbit no-one knows but it turned out to be an expensive day for both the dog and Mr Kirby!

Although Mr Kirby was not a candidate for membership of the RSPCA he seems to have managed his business quite well. The following is an extract from a local newspaper of the time:

Boon ploughing:-

Twenty-one of the neighbours of Mr Milner, the new tenant of Hawkshead Hall sent draughts a piece to assist him in putting in his grain on Wednesday. An excellent provision was made for them, at Mr Kirby's, the Kings Arms, in Hawkshead and a merry evening was passed after the work had been done.

Honey Pot

Just across the square from the Kings Arms is the Honey Pot. Unfortunately, to date little is known about this building. The frontage of the property is depicted in an oil painting of 1790 but lacks any real detail. It would appear from this painting that the upper windows have been added at a later date but exactly when is unsure. Before the turn of the last century it was owned by the Wilson family, along with two bakery buildings and an adjoining house, a barn and stable. The bakery was advertised as 'Wilsons' High Class Confectioner's and Baker's, Hawkshead'. Quite a wealthy family by all accounts, they also owned at that time, Laburnham House opposite and to the left the Kings Arms Hotel, along with other property at Roger Ground to the south-west of Hawkshead. All this land and property had been willed to two sisters and a brother, Miss Maggie Wilson and her younger brother ran the bakery business and the other sister Miss Cicelly worked as a teacher in the local school. By 1934 the Wilsons had sold the bakery premises to the Woolcock family who carried on as baker's and confectioner's until the 1950s. Between then and now it has belonged to four other families - Wright's, Femby's, Ball's and now the Taylforth's.

FOUNTAIN STREET TO ST MICHAEL AND ALL ANGELS

Fountain Street - Ross and Lantern Cottages (Eagle and Child Inn)

The public road to the left of the Honey Pot is known as Fountain Street. This is another picturesque corner of Hawkshead and leads round towards an old cobbled area, known as Slater's Yard. The two cottages facing the Market Square at the top of Fountain Street are called Ross and Lantern Cottages. Back in the 18th century this was said to be another inn, called the Eagle and Child. When the original building was split into two, is as yet unknown. Thankfully, one of the owners of the cottages today is keen to assist me with the identification of the Eagle and Child, so hopefully research into this building will start shortly.

Crumpet House

To the left of these cottages on the other side of Fountain Street can be found the first part of the town bakery. Look up and above the loft door you can see the original oak beam protruding from the wall with its iron hoop, with which they used to haul up the sacks of grain and flour into the second floor. There is a distinct line in the wall to the right, where an extension was added during the 1920s by the Wilson family. Looking straight ahead, you can see an arched building, this is the Crumpet House and was the second part of the bakery. The Crumpet House was basically used as a small separate bakery and storage area and was built in 1928 but before we discuss this building in detail if you look to the left you will find the 'Spout House'.

'Spout House'

The 'Spout House' is Hawkshead's main natural spring, which feeds several wells in the town, two of which we have just walked over in Fountain Street. There is only one well visible to the public in Hawkshead today and that can be seen through the back door of the Kings Arms Hotel. The spring at the Spout House has never been known to have dried up and has been the source of fresh water for the people of Hawkshead for centuries. For many years the buildings to the left of the Spout House were used as barns, sheds and haylofts, though the upstairs today, has been converted into a small flat, with its front door in the Spout House itself. These buildings are today owned by Hawkshead Co-Operative Society along with Rose Cottage in Fountain Street and other barns and buildings in the town.

Slater's Yard - Fern Cottage

Through the gap on the right we arrive in Slater's Yard, the last of Hawkshead's original cobbled areas. Slater's Yard gets its name from a man called John Slater, a local attorney at law, who had his business in what is now called Fern Cottage in the left hand corner of Slater's Yard. Besides being Mr Slater's office, this, back in the 18th and early part of the 19th century was the town jail or lock-up. The two jail cells are still to be found inside, although the property today is owned by the Kings Arms Hotel and is used as a holiday let.

Slater's Cottage

Next to Fern Cottage on the right stands Slater's Cottage, this is a fairly modern name as the cottage is a barn conversion. On the right-hand gable, can be seen

Slater's Yard 1880s. Buildings on right have gone. Left is back of Lantern and Ross Cottages

Mr Roland Shuttleworth

another cut-out section of the wall, used to allow the passage of a man with a horse. From here another entrance into Slater's Yard led, sloping downstairs into the bottom of the town beck in Flag Street. It was blocked up sometime in the last century.

Now looking to the left of Fern Cottage we arrive back at the Crumpet House. The building that used to stand on this site, was a large half-timber framed building pulled down in 1919, to make way for the present one. Like today's building, the original one had an archway on the left-hand wall, to allow access to the two cottages behind in the nook. Although the first arch was not as elaborate as the one of today, (for some peculiar reason this archway has been allowed to be blocked up, strange are the ways of local government!) The earlier building was built on the design of a typical early Hawkshead barn building, similar in design but on a much larger scale to the Beatrix Potter Gallery Ticket Office. The front and rear walls were of dry stone wall, while the two gables were made of a mixture of large upright flags at the base, above this were pegged walls and the top part of the gable was finished off with timber boarding. A flight of stone flag steps led up the outside of the building to the second floor.

The 'Nook'

With just behind them a row of outhouses which belongs to the two small cottages in the old Nook. Part of this row of outhouses has today been done away with to allow access into what remains of the Nook.

Church Hill (Cinder Path)

Turning around and entering Fountain Street again, on the right is a small 'weint' (passage) leading upwards behind the old bank building. Walking up the 'weint' brings us out at the top of, what is called Church Hill. The church on the summit, obviously supplies its name. But Church Hill does have an older name and that is, 'Cinder Path' but from where this originates is unsure.

Standing facing the church on the left, behind the Market House, are Hawkshead Church's two lych-gates (funeral gates). The one on the left is the original, made from two stone flags. In the olden days sheep were allowed to be kept in the churchyard to keep down the grass and the lych-gate was so designed as to allow the passage of a man fairly easily but if a sheep tried to escape, its rear haunches would get caught between the flags.

The main lych-gate was made at Hawkshead saw mill (the old monastery grain mill) in 1912 by Mr James Walker, the then proprietor. It was made with funds donated by the Boulton family, from New York, in America. They had visited Hawkshead trying to trace their roots and on finding that their ancestor Mr Giles Boulton had been an ex-headmaster of Hawkshead Grammar School, they left a sum of money with the church, to build the new lych-gate. There is a plaque attached to one of the main beams, which marks the occasion but unfortunately it is in a rather bad state of repair and is difficult to read.

Wordsworth House

Directly across from the lych-gates are another two properties, the last two dwelling houses on our tour and two of the most interesting. The one on the right is known as Wordsworth House and folklore has it that this is the property that nearly caught out Canon Rawnsley. Back then, like now, the locals tend to 'wind-up' the visitors and tourists in the pubs during the evenings. It would seem that Canon Rawnsley was no exception to the rule. The house at that time was up for sale and the owner and a friend were enjoying the 'chat' and a pint, at the bar of the Queens Head Hotel. Also standing at the bar was Canon Rawnsley. Knowing full well who he was and his 'near fanatical' interest with Wordsworth's days in Hawkshead, they started talking between themselves but just loud enough for Canon Rawnsley to overhear. Claiming that the house which was up for sale, was in fact William Wordsworth's lodgings in the town. His ears must have pricked up at this point, for they then went on to discuss the boxed in stream in the garden (this is actually part of the spring in the Spout House, where for a short length it appears on the surface of the ground). They got him hook, line and sinker and slowly reeled him in. Unfortunately, the Canon was not in the habit of buying property just on a whim but he did go on, so far as is known to write a paper on the subject. Never mind!

Wordsworth House and the one to the left, are two of only a few in Hawkshead to have cellars. The entrance to the cellar in Wordsworth House is to the right of the building, down the small alleyway. The building today has one bright yellow front door but originally it had two. If you look underneath the right-hand side of the downstairs window on the left, you can see underneath the pebbledash where it used to be. Back in the 18th century, Wordsworth House was another of Hawkshead's ale houses and this secondary door was used as the entrance. The interior of the property is quite interesting, it has two staircases, one on each inside gable, with a landing joining them at the back of the house. One local gentleman who was born there, remembers as a boy being chased by a local preacher (to whom he had been cheeky) into the house. To get away, he ran up one flight of stairs, across the landing, down the other flight of stairs and back out through the front door again, leaving the irate gentleman standing!

'Pillar Cottage' (Ivy Mount)

The building standing to the left of Wordsworth House is today called Pillar Cottage. It gets its name from the fact that the top floor comes forward from the main front wall and is supported by two stone pillars. The road now runs across the front of the building but originally, it ran underneath into a farmyard. Originally the property was built as a farmhouse but later on it was converted into two separate dwelling houses. Like Wordsworth House next door, it could well date back to the 15th century. Being a farmhouse it obviously had its own farm buildings, these can still be seen on the left. The barn has now been converted into a private house and the shippons and hayloft have been converted into a craft shop. The conversions took place in about 1968. Above the craft shop are the remains of a spinning or drying gallery. Leading up to the top floor of the barn from the farmyard was a set of stone flag steps, with a flagged off area at the bottom, which was used as a dung heap. This is where the old local name for Pillar Cottage came from, 'S... or Midden View'!

During the early 1900s the owner of Pillar Cottage or Ivy Mount as it was then known, was a Mrs Askew. She arrived in Hawkshead during the 1870s from west Cumberland and met and married her husband Edward Askew. He was the coachman for William Heelis (Beatrix Potter's husband) and Mrs Askew became their cook/housekeeper. She was affectionately known as 'old mother noo than'. This came from her strong Cumberland accent and 'noo than' means 'now then' and is still used today as a form of greeting, like 'hello'!

Mrs Askew was quite a remarkable lady known all around the area for her charity collections. Her granddaughter, Mrs Betty Ingham, from Grasmere still has her collecting box, which was a small red triangular box provided by the Methodist Society. The front of the box is inscribed as follows: Wesleyan Methodist Missionary Society 'The love of Christ constraineth' while the reverse has 'Gifts placed in this box are in aid of the foreign missionary work of the Wesleyan Methodist Church which includes: preaching the gospel, training the young in schools and colleges, sheltering the orphans, caring for the lepers, healing the sick and many other forms of Christian service'.

Over the years an exceptional amount of money passed through this little red box. After her death, at the funeral service, Reverend Walton announced that in her last year alone (1940) she had collected over £300. As you can appreciate this was no mean achievement back then.

Church of St Michael and All Angels

Now we shall visit the last major building on our tour of Hawkshead town, our Parish Church, situated on a small hillock to the south-west of the town but standing high above Hawkshead's rooftops, is the Church of St Michael and All Angels, the name by

Above: Farm buildings at Pillar Cottage with the spinning gallery on the right with Mrs Askew standing in front. Below is Pillar Cottage and Wordsworth House - both in 1930s   *Mrs E Ingham*

which it is still known today. It was suggested at one stage, that its original name was that of St Cuthbert's but this can not readily be proven. To the same extent its present name St Michael and All Angels, may only date back to the middle of the 18th century. But the first mention of chapelry here goes back to the 13th century, when the Archdeacon of Richmond was asked permission to 'hold mass with candles'. Obviously the building then looked nothing like it does today, as there have been many alterations and much rebuilding work carried out over the centuries. It would be pointless for me to list all alterations, as most of the details are available in the church itself. Inside the church as you enter from the north door, on the second set of pews, you will find some visitor boards, supplied by the Parochial Church Council, which are designed to give you an introduction and potted history of the church building. But here I will mention some of the main alterations as we go along. It would appear that the main body of the church is late 15th to early 16th century but the base of the tower walls could be even earlier, as they do not appear to be bonded into the main church walls. In 1578, the line of the roof was raised to allow extra light into the main nave and chancel. Most of the other alterations seem to have been inside the church, with the possible exceptions of it being re-roofed twice, once in 1756 and again in 1875. In 1793, when the church interior was re-pewed, the vestry was added to the north side of the tower. The last main addition to the building was in 1933 when local builder Mr George Usher, was tasked with adding the main north porch.

The churchyard on the north-eastern side of the building is the oldest part, although many of the gravestones have been removed. Some of these can still be found leaning against the south wall of the church itself. Over the years the churchyard has been expanded (more than doubled in size). During Wordsworth's days here in Hawkshead, the southern boundary was formed by a dry stone wall running from the Grammar School gates, up the hill towards where the beech hedge is today, with a five-barred wooden gate leading into the fields beyond and the Old Vicarage.

Saint Michael and All Angels 1900 - note the interlocking flag wall

Views from the Church

Some good views can be had of the town from Church End (eastern side of the church), looking out over Hawkshead to the meadows beyond. Here, running along the base of the wall, you will find a long stone seat, it originally ran right round the southern wall. This was the place where the local people would sit to hear the Parish Officers read out their notices. To the left of the stone seat above 'Jackie Steps', is the war memorial placed there to commemorate those who died in the two world wars from our parish.

Turning around, keeping the church on your right, follow the pathway round towards the church's southern entrance and from here you can see the more recent part of the churchyard, rising up to the top of the hill in front of you. Access to the top can be gained by either climbing the flight of steps in front of you or by taking a slow walk up the pathway on the right. From the top of the pathway, a gentle slope brings you out at the top of the churchyard. Arriving at the top, by whichever means, walk towards the low wall in front of you and from here there is an excellent panoramic view of the vale of Esthwaite. On the far right is Esthwaite Lake from where the valley gets its name, on the far left we have the Ambleside fells and directly opposite Latterbarrow, with its monument and Claife Heights stretching away towards Sawrey.

Priest Pot

From here, I will now describe the foreground starting with Esthwaite Lake on our right. Today the head of the lake finishes at the tree line of the small wooded area in the valley bottom, which is known as the Priest Pot. But long before Hawkshead was thought of, the lake bed stretched left. Over the years the valley bottom has silted up and is still doing so today at quite an alarming rate. About twenty years ago, core samples were removed from these fields to determine drainage problems and in those samples were found examples of freshwater life, that can still be found at the shoreline of Esthwaite Lake today.

The wooded area known as the Priest Pot is much overgrown and is very dangerous in parts, so it is to be avoided. The wood appears to float on water and in some places the ground is no more than a thin crust, it is in fact today a protected nature reserve but is not open to the public. In the northern most part of the wood is a large circle of water, this is the Priest Pot, at one time it was the private fishing grounds of the monks who were based at Hawkshead Hall. The monks were Cistercian Monks from Furness and Hawkshead Hall was the monastery, just to the north of the town.

Gibbet Moss

Looking beyond the Priest Pot there is a solitary tree standing on the side of the Sawrey road. All the fields to the left of this tree and surrounding the Priest Pot itself, are collectively known as Gibbet Moss. This was the site of a particular set of gallows erected solely for one purpose - to display the body of a local mass murderer, Thomas Lancaster.

Now Thomas Lancaster was not a native of the parish of Hawkshead, he originally came from Cumberland. He had met up with a local girl and decided that she was to become his wife. The fact that she was due to marry someone else did not come into it. Lancaster approached the girl's father and bribed him to stop the wedding and allow him (Lancaster) to marry the girl. The unfortunate deal was struck and on the 1st January, 1672 they were married and went to live on her father's farm at High Wray (two miles distant, beyond the top farm at the left of your view). For a few months everything bode well for them, then Lancaster started to show his true colours. With white arsenic, he poisoned his wife, her father, her three sisters, her former fiancè, her aunt and a servant boy. To make it appear as an epidemic of some sort, he then proceeded to poison his nearer neighbours, though they became seriously ill, they survived. He was duly arrested and placed before Sir Daniel Flemming of Rydal Hall, who committed him to the Assizes at Lancaster Castle, our county town. Here he was found guilty of mass murder and sentenced to death by hanging.

Lancaster was taken back to High Wray Farm, where he was hung by the neck from his own front door until he was dead. His body was then cut down and taken by horse and cart to the 'Poole Stang, at Hawkshead (the bridge on the Sawrey road on the outskirts of Hawkshead), where his body was hung in chains on the gibbet, until each bone dropped away from the other. A grisly end for an evil scheming man. The motive for these murders was to gain the family land and property. He died on 8th April 1672.

Now this is where the story of Thomas Lancaster should end, but right up until the 19th century, a strange story was told in connection with this gibbeting. In Hawkshead a cure was to be found for toothache, you would visit an old man in the town who owned a peculiar piece of wood, which had been handed down through his family. If you suffered from toothache he would cut a small sliver off, which you placed between your teeth. It was said to be guaranteed to work. What he failed to tell you was, that the piece of wood was part of the gibbet that Thomas Lancaster's body had dripped on. Ugh!

Looking straight ahead, on the far side of the valley, there is a farm known as Town End Farm, look slightly left and you will see a white building with a wall around it. This is the Friends Meeting House, built in 1688-89 and is part of the Quaker settlement of Colthouse. Looking slightly left is Colthouse proper. This is where the Wordsworth boys moved to with the Tysons. Green End Cottage can be found standing just to the right of the barn, which is on the extreme left of Colthouse. The cottage is owned by the National Trust but is not open to the public.

Look slightly left of the barn, two rows of hedges can be seen running north to south along the bottom of the valley. This is known as Scarhouse Lane (pronounced Skarus) and once formed the eastern shoreline of Esthwaite Lake. At some time in 1907, near the Colthouse end of the lane, some Roman coins were found by workmen repairing the footings of a wall and they were donated to the Ruskin Museum in Coniston. It has been supposed that Scarhouse Lane could well be part of an old Roman supply route between the main encampment of Galava Gate, near Ambleside and the Furness peninsular. Other Roman finds have been discovered in the area which could support this theory. There are the remains of a Roman house/villa on Borwick Ground Fell and a few remains of Roman brickwork at Hawkshead Hall.

Looking down, directly below us, is the Old School House, at Hickey Turnings, where we started our tour. So this is as good a point as any to finish off.

The author sincerely hopes that you have enjoyed your tour of our town.

John Dixon outside Methodist Chapel, Berkley Square, dressed in his 19th Century squire's attire ready to take people on a guided tour   *Phillip Bonney*

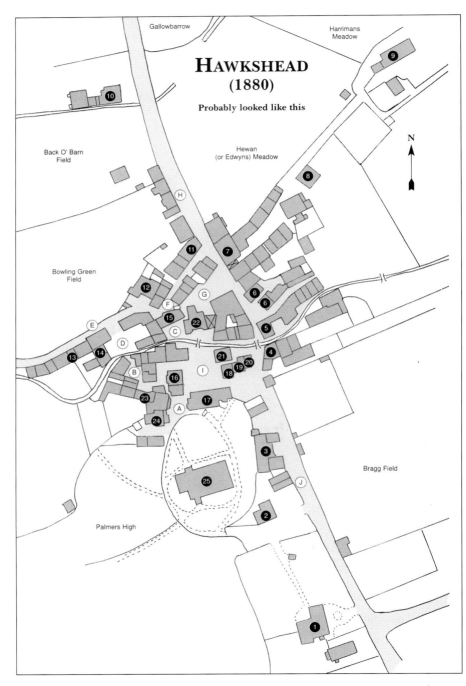

**HAWKSHEAD
(1880)**

Probably looked like this

Gallowbarrow

Harrimans
Meadow

Back O' Barn
Field

Hewan
(or Edwyns) Meadow

N

Bowling Green
Field

Bragg Field

Palmers High

KEY

1. Old School House
2. Grammar School
3. Sun Inn
4. Brown Cow Inn
5. Queens Head
6. Noble's Cottages
7. Red Lion Inn
8. Blacksmiths Shop
9. Black Beck Lodge
10. Greenbank
11. Farmhouse
12. Green End Cottage
13. Wee Cottage
14. Flag Cottage
15. Crown and Mitre
16. Shoe Shops
17. Market House
18. Tanners Arms
19. Tannery
20. Stable
21. Laburnham House
22. Kings Head
23. Town Spout
24. Pillar Cottage/Ivy Mount
25. St Michael and All Angels

A. Cinder Path
B. Slater's Yard
C. Berkley Square
D. Edward Statterthwaite's 'Usuall and Occupational Way'
E. Vicarage Lane
F. Grandy Nook
G. Red Lion Square
H. Main Street
I. Market Square
J. Church Stile

BIBLIOGRAPHY

'Wordsworth's Hawkshead' by T W Thompson, edited by Robert Woof

'Hawkshead (The Northernmost Parish of Lancashire): Its History, Archaeology, Industries, Folklore, Dialect, written in 1887 by H S Cowper

'Victorian and Edwardian Lake District from old photographs' Introduced and commentaries by J D Marshall and M Davies-Shiel

Barfoot and Wilkes Universal British Directory

The Westmorland Gazette

Lancashire Record Office

Barrow Record Office

Kendal Library

Private photographic collections

Most importantly the people of Hawkshead who have assisted me with their personal recollections, notes and information.

If you have enjoyed this book you may also enjoy other books published by Helm Press.

'A Westmorland Shepherd' *His life poems and songs*
'Elephants On The Line' *Tales of a Cumbrian railwayman (1947-95)*
'Dear Mr Salvin' *The story of the building of a 19th century Ulverston church*
'All In A Lifetime' *The story of a Dalesman as told to June Fisher*